Stories from the Globe

(Men's Edition)

Volume Two

Sharon Brown
(MO2VATE Magazine)

To Lama,

Love you loads,

Daddy

xxxx

To Laura,

Love you loads,

Dad
xxxx

Published by The Book Chief Publishing House 2022
(a trademark under Lydian Group Ltd)
Suite 2A, Blackthorn House, St Paul's Square, Birmingham,
B3 1RL
www.thebookchief.com

Book Cover Design: Deearo Marketing
Editor / Proofreader: Laura Billingham
Coordinator / Proofreader: Nicola Matthews
Typesetting / Proofreading / Publishing: Sharon Brown

THE BOOK CHIEF®
IGNITE YOUR WRITING

TABLE OF CONTENTS

DEDICATION

To all of the amazing men all over the world who are fighting some incredible battles and pushing through the toughest of challenges to create a life they love.

FOREWORD

By Adam Claxton

When I first came across MO2VATE Magazine, little did I know just how much of an impact this magazine would have on my life.

I am a great believer in the Law of Attraction and how opportunity aligns itself at the right time and MO2VATE Magazine was the platform that leveraged my journey not only as a featured article writer, but now as a co-author alongside some fantastic individuals that took the leap of faith to write about their life stories.

When I submitted my first article based on Gratitude, I had doubts over my own ability, but the team behind the scenes are amazing at supporting and unleashing peoples' true potential.

This has led me to many more opportunities and I for one am grateful that this book, Stories from around the Globe (Men's Edition) has come to fruition. It comes in a time where the world has changed and as we adapt to this new phase of life, Stories from around the globe will help support, guide and inspire you to take responsibility for yourself and work on areas of your life that you would like to see change.

There is nothing more motivating that working with a collective of men that have all shared their stories, from mental health illness, striving and thriving in business and turning negative situations into positives.

They say that everybody has a story to tell and situations in life push us to make decisions that better our futures. When you are ready to start your book journey or if you fancy becoming the next front cover of a magazine, make sure it is MO2VATE Magazine that you feature in. Always strive to be the best version of you.

INTRODUCTION

This book highlights the life journeys of 10 inspirational men from different parts of the world, who have faced challenges that could easily have set them back in life, but instead they used their experiences to push themselves forward and create a life they choose.

We hope this book speaks to those who are currently going through challenges and allows them to realise there is light at the end of the tunnel. Persistence and determination and the sheer will to get through challenges is what has driven these Authors to where they are in life now and they want you to know, you can do it too.

Thank you for purchasing a copy of this book.

CHAPTER 1

Why I am Here

By Adam Claxton

It was not until I was four days away from getting married that I knew I had to make meaningful changes. This was in October 2014, and with just four days to go, I made the toughest but best decision of my life. I was 32 years old and could see the rest of my life being so much different if, for once, I followed my heart instead of going through with the wedding and living a life not being true to myself.

I had made the decision to call it off and knew there would be mixed feelings due to the number of people that I had let down, the thoughts and judgements of others, committing to do something that I did not want to do. But most importantly, I was being honest with myself as I did not see a life of happiness in front of me if I turned up for the special day.

You can imagine how it must have gone down, but I just kept hold of my thoughts and feelings about the future.

No matter how hard things would get, I knew I had done the right thing.

For years I had lost my sense of purpose; I was stuck in a dead-end job even though there were days that I enjoyed it. I did not feel like this was the life I was going to live until I reached the retirement age.

In the relationship, I had lost touch of my original self, often finding myself people pleasing, being something that I was not, and putting others wellbeing before my own. One of the hardest things to say is that I lost me.

I was a lost soul, going through life in the comfort zone, but I knew I had the potential for much more.

Shortly after calling the wedding off, I decided it was time to hand in my notice. I had worked in retail for a well-known supermarket for 16 years. Working my way through the ranks from a young age, I finished as a Security Manager.

For years I knew that I did not want to work there for the rest of my life, but the comfort zone was a tough place to get out of. I had a steady income, holiday pay, sick pay, pay rises, shares, and it worked comfortably around my work/life balance.

At the same time, I had started doing extra security work to keep my mind active and have another source of income which opened my eyes massively to the world. One day I would be stopping shoplifters the next day, I was on the red carpet of Leicester Square looking after the rich and famous.

This was such an awakening moment for me, and going back to my day job on the Monday just did not suffice.

It was time to pursue my own happiness and see what I could make of life.

I started doing more security work with the aim of having my own business, but it was not that easy. I enjoyed the work I was doing from film premieres, film and TV sets, sporting events, VIP, Royal Parties and much more.

During this time, I had my first encounter with my mental health.

I have always tried to stay healthy and often train where I have a passion for martial arts and, in particular, Muay Thai. This martial art helped me to regain my confidence; it allowed me to focus and understand the power of my mindset and built resilience which would come in handy.

There were days that I just did not have any motivation; it had just disappeared, I struggled to leave the house, and I felt like I was not worthy of being here. I just could not switch off from what my mind was thinking and how I was feeling.

I was feeling flat, depressed, and anxious about the future. I had worries about finances as the security work was not coming in as thick and fast as I would have liked it to, and I doubted my capabilities. I often wondered whether I had made the right decision to leave my career.

In my spare time, I would watch motivational videos on YouTube, which often left me feeling upbeat and inspired to achieve more. I studied all things that fascinated me, such as the law of attraction, spirituality, numerology, mindset, and I recognised feeling much more positive every time I focused on these subjects.

I recognised that when I focused my energy on working on more elements of my wellbeing, I was able to achieve more. Combining my mental, physical, spiritual, and emotional health was the recipe to not only help rebuild myself mentally but, over time, allowed my soul to repair.

In 2017 I went on a business course in Birmingham, and one of the things that stood out most was the coach saying, "Follow your passion it will lead you to your purpose."

This stuck in my mind and got me thinking; my passion was Muay Thai, but how do I turn that into making money?

I spoke with my friend and asked him if he would pay to come and punch me.

"When?" was his reply.

That was it; my business was born.

We trained, and with the power of social media, I was able to advertise what I was doing. It was not long before I started meeting new people from all levels of society that were coming to train with me.

I put clients through their paces using Muay Thai style workouts and pad work and helped people become better versions of themselves. I coached my clients to improve their mindset and focus on the positives in life; I listened to what they had to say then challenged them to make better choices which led them to feeling better not just physically but mentally.

Through word of mouth, social media and me talking about what I was doing, I was really making a difference, especially to those that suffered with their mental health. Clients would say I was their therapist, life coach and guru as I shared my knowledge, understood what people were feeling with my gift as an empath and found solutions for people's issues.

From this, I trained in Cognitive Behavioural Therapy, Life Coaching and much more to equip myself even more so I could help more people.

I have helped people to live more purposefully, escape toxic relationships, and have turned people's lives around when suicide looked to be the only way out. I've helped others to understand the importance of self-care, our wellbeing, and I share the things that I did when I was in a dark place.

Sitting here now, I can honestly say that when I lost everything, I found myself.

As the years in business went by, I still felt like I had more to give and hosted an event where I took to motivational speaking, using my story to inspire others to want to make changes and have a positive impact on people's lives.

It was a calling, and something intuitive came to me saying that I had to evolve and push myself further. I constantly challenge myself out of my comfort zone as I know too well what happens when you stay in it for too long.

In 2020 as the Coronavirus pandemic hit the world, the physical business I had spent years building almost ended instantly. Restrictions and rules stopped what I was doing, but it was also another blessing.

As somebody who looks for the positives in every situation, I was able to rebuild and move into an online market as I can make a bigger difference to the world once again.

With the pandemic and people suffering alone with their mental health, I knew that going online with business would allow me to affect the world on a wider scale.

I started to make regular features on a Psychic Radio show giving insights and spreading my positivity, featured on mental health-based podcasts again sharing my story, hoping that it can inspire those that might need to hear what I have to say. I now make regular features in MO2VATE Magazine, where I cover topics from Gratitude to Manifestation and continue delivering my mantra of all things mindset, motivation, and mental health.

In February 2021, Ex-special forces and number one selling author Ant Middleton (SAS- Who Dares Wins) commended me for my brave decision that started my journey of self-discovery. It reminded me that anything is possible when you put your mind to it and step out of the ordinary to pursue your purposeful mission.

If you are reading this today, I want you to know that you can and will turn your life around when you decide to turn up for yourself, set good routines and have good people around you that can motivate you when the days are tough.

For me, our wellbeing consists of four elements mental, physical, emotional, and spiritual.

Start by taking time every day to train these elements just as much as you would train yourself physically.

When I was at my lowest point, I realised that as strong as I was physically; mentally, emotionally, and spiritually I was miles away from where I needed to be. To get myself back to me, I had to find balance in my wellbeing, and this is what prompted me to explore, learn and most importantly, put into action the new behaviours I had learnt.

One of the most important things we can do to improve our mental and emotional health is to talk about how we are feeling. For years this had not been the case; I masked my true emotions and replaced them with focusing on Muay Thai; alcohol helped to numb the pain and just coming from a place where it was easier not to say anything to keep all other parties happy at the detriment to my own happiness. I began to work on my mindset by reprogramming the way I thought and focusing on positivity. I listened to what I was saying, then corrected that thought as the power of what we think multiplies once it has been said.

I explored avenues of spirituality and found great peace in meditation, again breaking a stigma attached to what I originally believed or felt due to the views and opinions of others. What other people think has a massive impact on what you do, but what if you were to just try doing these things so you know and can produce your own opinion?

Meditation helped me to become more mindful and allowed me to truly focus my energy on the present moment. We only have what we have in front of us right now and quite often take the next breath for granted. In a fast-paced world, we can lose ourselves. Having a moment to be more mindful can make such a positive impact to regain clarity in our decision making and bring us back to the here and now.

Give yourself time to grow, set goals and find ways to achieve them.

Look after yourself, speak more positively about your life and remember that you have survived 100% of your down days.

Always strive to become the best version of yourself. This is my story; this is me.

CHAPTER 2

Mindset is Everything!

By Dean Fox

I am sure you have all heard this quote many times, I know I had, but I took it with a pinch of salt until I really experienced how it can impact your life and business. When we understand that 95% of our actions are driven by our subconscious mind, in other words, we actually only have conscious control of 5% of our daily actions, we realise how powerful the mind really is.

I hope that my journey and the experiences I share with you will not only inspire you but really show that by changing your mindset, you can literally change your life!

Where It All Started.

It's 1983, and I am sitting in the dressing room before an important junior football match. The air was filled with the smell of Deep Heat spray and the sound of excited chatter and banter, and the sound of studs tapping on the tiled floor.

I had all the usual pre-match mix of butterflies and excitement!

There was a hush as the coach came into the dressing room, holding the team sheet for the game; he started reading out the names…and my name wasn't on it!

Wait…I was the leading scorer; how come I wasn't playing?

Maybe I wasn't as good as I thought I was?

And there it was, the underlying self-doubt that was lurking, waiting for every opportunity to show me "the truth" that I believed.

From that day on, I became this "over achiever" and go to work to try and prove "I am good enough", whether that's in sport, academics, career, or business.

So I really work hard, and by the time I am 32, I am the National Sales Manager for a major PLC with an expense account, company car and a multi 7 figure budget.

But the inner critic never left; it continued to remind me that maybe "I wasn't good enough", and I continued to suffer from imposter syndrome.

I kept feeling that I was capable of more, but it was like there was something holding me back, like driving with the handbrake on. I felt like I was on a hamster wheel or treadmill, and things just always seemed to be a struggle.

I had developed what I now call a "When-Then" mentality; when I have done this, then I will be happy/successful /good enough; when we live in this house/drive this car/earn this much…

The trouble was the "then" never came, I still felt exactly the same way, so I would simply set another "when.

This wasn't just physically tiring but emotionally and mentally exhausting!

When I have my own business

I came to the conclusion that I would feel successful, happy, good enough if I had my own successful business.

This was my next "when" …

So, when the company I was working for was restructuring, I decided to make the jump into entrepreneurship and set up a property business with my wife.

I believed this was the opportunity to not only grow a successful business but to prove I was "good enough" once and for all! It was hard work, but by the time I was 36, we had grown a successful multi 6 figure business, built our dream home, drove our dream cars, and went on dream holidays.

Things were going well, so well in fact, we invested some of our funds with a company we were introduced to through our property contacts.

However, even though we were happy at times and enjoyed what appeared to be a successful life, I still had that feeling of "self-doubt", the idea that "things are going too well, there must be something about to happen"!

I didn't understand that I was actually willing this into existence, attracting it, that my thoughts were actually bringing this into reality.

The Financial Crash

In 2008 we were just about to secure a deal for our biggest and most ambitious development yet, one that would have a development value of in excess of £1.5m and take our business over the 7-figure mark. We had also planned a huge family trip to Australia for almost a month to celebrate.

There had been rumours and one or two signs in early 2008 that some problems were emerging in the financial markets, and in September 2008, as we prepared for our "trip of a lifetime", everything came crashing down.

The property market crashed, the financial sector that we relied on so heavily, imploded.

The institutions who provided our funding pulled our lines of credit; some of them wanted outstanding loans back, almost with immediate effect!

Our days of that trip, which was supposed to be a huge family celebration of success, were spent on the phones, trying to negotiate extensions, minimise losses and keep the doors open. To make matters worse, the company we partnered with to invest our profits turned out to be a fraud!

By the end of 2009, everything seemed to be crumbling around us, every day was a struggle, and we felt like we were fighting a losing battle. I decided that in order to steady the ship and keep us afloat, I would go back and get a job in the Sales sector again.

A different type of Crash

Sunday 28th March 2010 was a day that impacted my family and me in so many ways.

"I don't like this…I feel really vulnerable…"
These were the last words I heard from my wife as we approached a busy junction in the car on our way to a junior football game.

Seconds later, there was a huge bang, and everything went black…

It was several minutes before I started to come to.

I couldn't work out what was happening...

My vision was blurred, sounds were distorted, and I was drifting in and out of consciousness.

The next time I came round, I recall a man leaning in the car through the passenger window and asking if I was OK?

I still couldn't figure out what was happening; I slipped back into the darkness...

My memory of events of that day has many gaps, and I lost all sense of time. There are moments I can remember vividly, but many "memories" are simply made up from the recollections of others who were there that day.

The accident was a major incident, the road we were travelling on would remain closed for almost 5 hours, and it would be over 2 hours before they were able to cut us from the car.
My son had to be airlifted to hospital as they had real concerns that he may lose a leg, and my wife and I suffered numerous broken bones and fractures and a punctured lung.

These injuries, hospitalisation, surgery, and the months of physiotherapy meant my plan of going back to get a job to help "steady the ship" was impossible.

With the mounting financial pressures and the inability to work during that time, I ended up bankrupt, and we lost all the cars and property and were in danger of losing our home!

I began to really struggle with my mental health; each day I felt like I was getting out of bed and climbing into a swimming pool to swim all day against the current; I was physically and mentally exhausted.

There were days when I didn't want to even get out of bed; I struggled to explain what I was going through to my wife and family. I told myself, "they had enough to deal with", and I didn't want to burden them with my struggles.

In December 2010, I reached my lowest point; I woke up one Sunday morning, it was a cold but bright winters day, and I said to my wife that I was going to go for a walk, to clear my head and think about what I could do to find a way through all this

That was a lie…
The truth was, as I left the house that morning and walked to some woodland near our home, I had no intention of coming home…

The day that changed my life

Why me?

Why am I going through this?

Those were the thoughts that were running through my head as I stood in the woodland near my home contemplating ending my life.

I was depressed and really struggling; I thought my family and the world would be a better place without me. I felt alone, I felt disappointed in myself, I felt this was all my fault, I felt like I had done so many times before…that I just wasn't good enough!

I was angry, with myself, with the world, with everyone, but I was also sad and in pain…I just wanted it all to go away.

With tears streaming down my face, I made the decision that there was only one way out, and that was to take my own life.

But…

Something strange happened.

In the middle of all those emotions, I suddenly felt a real calm descend over me…

It was as if someone had "lifted" all that stress, worry, fear, and pain and just gave me a moment to reflect without feeling any of those things.

I don't know how long that lasted, but it was so peaceful

One overriding thought kept coming up, time and time again, I could have died nine months ago; in fact, everyone who witnessed that day in March said, "nobody should have survived ", but I did.

Why was that? Why have I had to go through all this since?

I didn't get the answers to those questions that day, but I did get an overwhelming urge to find the answers, and that was what "brought me back that day."

A decade of learning

There were times in my life when I did something, and then someone asked, "why did you do that"?

"I don't know", I would often reply.

Sometimes I might even know that I shouldn't have done it, but I couldn't figure out why I still did.

Ever experienced that yourself?

Well, I wanted to figure out those reasons and understand how to take the actions I wanted and stop doing the things that weren't serving me.

So, I committed to invest in myself, to learn everything I could about the mind and human potential, to understand why I did the things I did, why I believed the things I did and more importantly, why I found it difficult sometimes to do the things I wanted or even knew I should be doing!

I have worked with many amazing mentors and coaches and learned from some phenomenal people, but the number one thing I have learned is that when we can change what we think and believe about ourselves and the world, then we can change our lives!

Since I discovered this information and started implementing it into my life, everything changed for me.

My wife and I joined a Network Marketing business, and together we grew it to be in the top 2% of the organisation; I became a national trainer for the organisation too.

I set up a new international consulting company and grew it to 6 figures within 18 months from a standing start.

I started a coaching and speaking business, and I have delivered keynotes to thousands of people at both live and virtual events and have coaching clients from all over the world.

If you're reading this, then I am now also a published author, another dream that I had; I have also appeared on numerous podcasts and been interviewed for local and international press.

I have travelled to South East Asia, India, the Middle East, the USA and across Europe, and seen places that have truly taken my breath away, like the Taj Mahal and the Grand Canyon. I have met amazing people and experienced phenomenal cultures, and this has all been down to the transformation I made in my life.

The reason I wanted to share my journey, the good and the bad, the highs and the lows, with you, is I wanted you to know that despite where you are right now, despite your current results, anything is possible for you.

See, your current results are not a reflection of your potential; your current results are simply a reflection of everything you have thought and believed up to this point; your potential is unlimited!

Once you commit to changing your thinking and mindset, then you can literally achieve anything; nobody could have convinced me of this previously, despite my successes.

However, I am now utterly convinced that what I have achieved (and so much more) is available to absolutely anyone, including YOU!

Mindset truly is everything!!

CHAPTER 3

Beyond 'Why?' A search for meaning

By Ian Llewellyn Nash

I did not see it coming, I was reasonably fit. True, I overindulged on occasions, and my lifestyle had become more sedentary than my prior life of implicit fitness as a member of Her Majesty's Armed Forces. As a Royal Navy medic, I did need to be capable of running and getting in and out of spaces. At school, I was the 100-metre champion, which extended to the County. I enjoyed fitness and playing football - I achieved a cupboard full of Cup Winner medals. That had dissipated in the world of work. However, to all appearances, all was well with this mortal frame.

After leaving the Royal Navy, I was employed as a Registered Nurse in my local hospital. I was by then a senior nurse on the Coronary Care Unit, and I also undertook a lecturing role with the Open University.

Additionally, I was part of the wider Leadership Team at my local church. Prior to that, I had been the Pastor of a rural church in a nice village setting that experienced growth and development whilst I was there. Alongside this, I was a father to four children. Life was busy.

A casual visit to the church building was accompanied by an ever-increasing amount of pain in my right loin area (that is, the right side of my back).By the time I got home, which was a 5-minute drive, I was doubled over in pain and literally crawling on all fours to survive. My General Practitioner - a lovely doctor, called at my home and alleviated my pain with morphine, then sent me off to the hospital with a diagnosis of kidney stones. Whether that was a trigger for what then followed remains a talking point at one level, at another a reference in time for the onset of signs and symptoms over a space of six weeks which would change my life forever and put me at risk of early death.

Within the space of six weeks, due to circumstances and laboratory tests, I was diagnosed with a rare blood disorder. A disorder that was incurable and opened the door to many life-threatening complications and at the time held a prognosis of around ten to twelve years. I would be sustained by three weekly blood transfusions. That enabled me to keep working. In hindsight, that was probably a good thing as I found myself having to come to terms, or at least my wife and I had to initially confront the reality, that everything was now in a state of upheaval and doubt and I would not experience the joy of seeing my children get married, or have their own children.

As a father, I would not walk my girls down the aisle or proudly show off my son. On a more practical level: what about the debts, the bills, how would my wife and children get by?

I did not see that coming!

Those that know me will usually attest to me being a quiet person. Solid, dependable, stubborn, stoic. I am often criticised for not talking a lot; on this occasion, I struggled to find any words. Plans, aspirations, hopes, dreams for the future were stationary at a red light.

Just the everyday reality of living was thrown into a thick cloud with scant to zero visibility of emerging out of the other side.

It was perhaps inevitable then that eventually, during one dark night of the soul, the grumbling, rolling, ever-increasing pain inside me found a voice and shouted out the question: Why? Why has this happened? Why? Why? Why?

I'm not the first to ask such questions; I doubt that I will be the last. For myself, the thing that brought all this pain and doubt and anger into stark relief was that I was a person of faith. I was a church leader. A teacher and Pastor in the church. The previous year I had made a second visit to Albania to undertake aid mission work. I should find solace in my faith.

Well...I didn't! Not for quite a while. Telling those nearest and dearest to me that I was on a journey that was going to end in an early death was not easy - especially my children.

I'm not in that place any longer. Yes, there are times when I do still get angry at God, at life, when I feel inhibited by this illness that seeks to impact my life. However, I don't live there anymore. I moved beyond the 'why'.

There is a story told by the writer of the book we refer to as John's Gospel (Chap 9:1-3), which tells the story of a sick person who comes to Jesus for healing. Some of the disciples focus not so much on the state that this person was in but on the causation.

Why is this person sick? Is it because of something he did? Jesus, in addressing their questioning, replied: (my paraphrase) "Guys, you got this all wrong. It's not about 'why'. It's about 'what now'! Listen, we can chat and debate about why this person has this illness, was it his fault or his parents?

That is not the issue. The issue is what can we do now to move this person forward out of his present state to something more meaningful". Jesus healed the person who then went on to live his life.

'What now…?'

The 'why' question had become, for me, an unhelpful focus. It was an accusative focus directed at the object of my faith. I came to discover that there is a better question: what now? It's not a question asked in desperation or confusion. It's a question directed at the resourcefulness of the human condition, of health, of healing, of, in my context, faith.

My focus shifted beyond why did this occur to what can I do now? What does this require of me now?

What ways can I show up in the world now? What does looking forward instead of backwards add to my journey now? The longer I kept myself at the level of the accusatory why question, the longer I would be treading water.

Moving beyond 'why' and adopting a 'what now' disposition enabled me to stand on the other side of fear and adopt principles that got me out of stasis and moved me forward. Principles that I have used since in my teaching, in my coaching practice and in my own ongoing living. On this journey, I identified three principles that enabled me to gain a sense of balance and purpose in getting up from the situation I had found myself in.

We react to what we do not understand

Andrew Smith (2014), in his book, 'Minha metade silenciosa' (My Silent half), wrote the following words: "People fear what they cannot understand and what they cannot control."

There have been a lot of events in my life that have been unsettling and caused anxiety. For example, getting into debt in my early years of marriage, losing my job on several occasions.

Yet, these were external events, and to a degree, there was a way out of such occasions. The diagnosis of my blood disorder and the prognosis at that time of a life span of some 10- 12 years was heart-crushing, immobilising and left me devastated as I had no frame of reference. Internally, I was isolated, and I felt alone, scared, hurt and angry.

Fundamentally, I feared all the consequences; I was also struggling with my personal faith. I mean, I had been a church leader, I had seen people healed of illnesses, the deaf hearing, the blind seeing, the infertile giving birth - yet I crumbled in the face of something which I did not understand - why me? - and I could not control. I did not have to live there. Knowledge and understanding could be gained.

Live from a present-future orientation

Laying in a hospital bed attached to a haemodialysis machine as a result of being in kidney failure, I saw a young woman walk into the ward to receive her weekly dialysis. She wore a T-Shirt with the words printed on the front: 'Feel the fear and do it anyway'.

Those words had a huge impact on my thinking and then on how I chose to respond to my situation. It was Susan Jeffers in her 2007 book of the same name who originally wrote these words.

Her book was aimed at people who were living their lives in stasis due to fear. For example, fear of asserting oneself; making decisions; being alone; intimacy; ageing; ill health; ending a relationship; losing a loved one; failure.

Most often, as individuals, we tend to live our lives from the perspective of the present, using the past as a reference point. What is happening to me now, my experiences now, are all because of something that happened in the past. Past debt, past doubt, past illness, a past diagnosis. Living present-past can be inhibiting. In contrast, to live present-future is empowering, positive and enabling. To live present-future takes into consideration the hope embodied in the shift from the accusative 'why me' question, to the affirming, 'what now' question. A reorientation to hope without which living is futile.

—

'What now' empowers others where they are the 'why' question had me stuck in a place of despair. I could not see a way out, nor a way through. The shift to the 'what now' question was illuminating. It offered hope, and hope offered a way through. Hope offered purpose. The 'what now' question got me out of a personal downward spiral and re-positioned me to a place of recovery.

Asking the 'what now' question also took the focus of myself and placed it onto others: those around me. My family. My work colleagues. My friends - all of whom had stood with me in various ways as my health and vitality had declined.

To ask of myself, 'what now' was to accept that there was an option to sitting, moping around, and feeling sorry for myself, or accepting that I had a condition, rather than a condition having me. My focus shifted from me in my world to me in a world of others, others whom I could still enjoy and add value to.

The context of this story is that of a health challenge. It is my hope that you have found that encouraging and informative. However, the principles that I share are good for a wide range of life situations, be that personal, professional, even domestic. I'm a strong advocate of the principle that if what we share does not lead to or provoke change, then all we have shared is information.

Some practical applications from this story:

Asking 'why' when in the accusative will keep you stuck. Ask a better question.

Ask 'what now' as this will shift you from using the past as a point of reference and shift you to a future orientation in which new ways of thinking and doing can emerge.

It's not all about you. Unless you are a hermit, your life will touch and be touched by others - make those touchpoints positive ones - for life is but a short adventure.

What now shifts you beyond the futility of life to the fruitfulness of life.
Footnote:

Due to advances in medicine and drug therapy, I am now +12 years from my original expected year of expiration. I breathe deeply each day, and I am joyful that each day offers a new 'what now'?

CHAPTER 4

The Story Unfolds

By John Reed

April 21st. 1948, the Queen's birthday, and my mums birth day, the day I was born. I was her first child after three years of marriage, and she took me home to the rooms that she and my father shared in Staines, Middlesex.

As I sit here writing this piece, the story unfolds easily to me, and so let me take you on the journey from 1948 until 1970. The changes were many in this post-war period, and I wonder if my parents worried for my future in the same way I now worry for the future of my children and grandchildren.

In 1948 there were a number of important dates. That year the Olympic games were held in London; although I do not remember them, however, they must have been very different to the games or 2012.

Also, that year in July, the NHS was established. Had this been in place before my birth, then things would have been much cheaper for my mum. Private Healthcare had to be paid for, and my mum would not have found this easy.

And this situation highlights a major feature of life today. The NHS has been a lifeline for my generation, and I really am not sure how we would have coped with a pandemic in those pre-1948 days.

Of course, over this period, how medicine has transformed everyone's life has changed fundamentally and methods, equipment, and training have assisted in this change. For my part, I have benefited greatly from the improvements to our Healthcare System. I am fortunate that, to date, I have not experienced any serious illness, but as one gets older, the need for support becomes greater, and who knows what the future holds for me.

Consider also the education system, which has changed radically in my lifetime. I began my schooling at the age of five in 1953. It was a three-school system, infants, junior and senior, and I left school aged 15 in 1963. I sat no exams and therefore had very little choice of career. The career advisor persuaded me to become a gas fitter (they do not exist anymore), and so my five-year apprenticeship began.

In those days we travelled between jobs on bicycles! We had no mobile phones, no calculators, or mechanisation of any kind, and we worked in an environment where health and safety were not high on the priority list.

Looking back, I wonder how the younger people would fare today. Indeed I wonder how the customers would feel if they received the speed of response today that we offered in the 60s. Can you imagine smelling gas in your house and the men arriving on a bicycle! Of course, the risks were great, but that was life then.

In the period from 1960 until 1970, the world saw many changes, societal, economic and political; however, at the time, I did not fully comprehend what the outcomes could be. Society changed for a variety of reasons, mostly in a liberal direction. Birth control allowed unwanted pregnancies to be avoided, and many argued that this would lead to promiscuity. However, the beginning of a liberation movement for women, equality, tended to argue the opposite and looking back, I think I agree with the equality. For me, it is impossible to argue against sexual equality, and I think the world is a better place today than it was then.

But society changed in many other ways, not least the world of music. I remember programmes on TV like "Top of the Pops" and "Ready, Steady, Go," which changed the way in which people of my age listened to music. As is usual, my parents reacted as I do now, they were not that keen and thought the words were "unintelligible" and "far too loud", so perhaps nothing changes!

With liberation came changes to the way in which we dressed. This was true for both men and women, and whereas women had always dressed smartly, men not so much. For men like me, pointed shoes (winkle pickers), slim fit trousers (drain-pipe by trousers), and colourful shirts transformed our appearance. I'm sure that sociologists can write book after book on this change to society, but for me, it was just another step in growing up.

Similarly, for women, the changes were profound. The hem on a skirt rose, and legs became much more of a feature than they had been previously. In the early part of the century, dress lengths were very long, and it was thought that the sight of an ankle was not good, that it was a bit risqué. As time progressed, hems were raised, and so for many, miniskirts were a natural development. Colours also became brighter, styles became more important, and all of these factors helped develop the world of equality.

These were the days when young men like me wanted to see the world. I had travelled with my school to Italy in 1961, and many years later I travelled much further than this for my work, and this desire to travel is still with me today. But in 1964, aged 16, I could buy and ride a motor scooter, and this gave me my freedom. But not for long; within three months, I crashed and found myself in hospital, thank goodness for the NHS. One year later, at 17, I bought my first car and from then on never looked back.

Of course, the cars were also nothing like the cars of today. Technically inferior, less safe, less environmentally friendly, and prone to breaking down often. But I liked my car because it gave me freedom, and at that age, at that time, it was the men who sought to influence the women. Put simply, it was not the case that generally girls asked boys out; the opposite was true. And so my car was exactly what was needed to find a girlfriend, who hopefully would become my wife.

Political changes also shaped my world. Governments come, and Governments go, and so it will remain for all time, and until 1970 these changes had little effect on my life. But undoubtedly, due to these changes, my life also changed along with the changes to society, and so the world in which I lived was very different, especially when compared with today. In simple terms, a Conservative Government seems to attract the more affluent of the population, whereas a Labour Government helps the working class. This is probably an oversimplification; however, it is the view that I had at these times.

It should be noted that there was no teaching of politics, law, economics, even sex in school at that time, and so I and all my friends made our own minds up based on what we read in the newspapers, and what we saw on television, radio news was irrelevant as we did not listen to it. Nowadays, all of these topics are openly discussed on TV, radio, and social media, so today's younger people have a much better opportunity to form opinions than we had.

This, of course, has a major influence on the way the world interacts because the western world has a much different view to the rest of the world, and this often leads to conflict. The question therefore is clear, is the world a better place today than in the period under discussion?

Let us return to the main topic of this piece. My life experience during this time was shared with many other people of my age. We had no idea of what was to come, how the world would develop, and how our lives would be affected. The pattern of life was very simple, five years at home, ten years at school, 50 years at work. I had no plans other than to grow up, get married, have a family, and work until retirement, aged 65.

But was this realistic even then? Probably not, but I had no way of visualising what my future might become. There was no encouragement from family or friends to allow me to consider what life prospects I might enjoy if I chose a different path. My father said, "you need a trade, John and we need your income to help the family", and so leaving school, taking an apprenticeship and qualifying seemed to be the obvious goal.

Would my life be different if I were 16 today? Of course, yes, but how different is the question. I am sure that I would have gone to university aged 18, not as I actually did aged 45.
This would have had a profound effect on my life; perhaps I would have become a professional person rather than a skilled person. But would this have made me any happier in my life? There is, of course, no answer to this question because we cannot go back in this life, only forwards.

I began writing this piece and intended that I should look back over my life from 1948 until 1970. However, as I write this, I realise one cannot look back on just one part of one's life in isolation because those formative years have shaped my whole life.

Without those first 22 years, I would not be the person I am today. In 1970 I married for the first time, and my wife and I brought two sons into the world in the 1970s. In the early eighties, we divorced, and I remarried, and none of this could I foresee in my early years.

Many people now argue that to be successful in life, you need a plan. I had a plan, but it was one that was based on expectations rather than hope and this, in my now experienced opinion, was wrong. Hope grows eternal, and hope gives us aspirations, and nowadays I find my aspirations are my motivation, and I see no reason why this should not be so. At my age, many people have already retired from the world of work, but I have no intention of so doing. Currently, I work part-time in a sector that I was totally unaware of in the early years of my life. That being the case, how could I have possibly planned to be where I am today?

I will end this piece at this point because I can see that what I set out to write is not what I have actually written. This dichotomy reflects my whole life; that which I have found to be most satisfying in my life could not have been foreseen. When I planned my working life, I had no idea of what sectors there may be for me to explore. And so, education would have helped me if only I had allowed it to. It is too easy to say my father forced me into work; he did not, but he did encourage me to leave education, and that is something I have never done to my children.

Am I bitter? Not at all. Life is what you make it. I just think it is a shame that my life today did not come at a younger age because if it had, I would have enjoyed my working life all the more.

CHAPTER 5

Life Can Change in a Split Second

By Kyle N. Scott

Whether you're disabled or able-bodied, we're all faced with the challenges life can unfairly throw our way. Trying to achieve our goals amidst these hurdles drives us to push beyond what we thought possible in pursuit of those dreams. Some of us thrive in those situations while others retreat. As someone who is wheelchair-bound and living with cerebral palsy, what matters at the end of the day is that we tried our best and can fondly look back at how we overcame adversity.

An hour before my birth in 1989, my life was in jeopardy. With my heart thumping at a critically low 33 BPM, my mother was rushed into an emergency C-section. There it was discovered that I was asphyxiating on meconium, a condition often fatal in the delivery room. Even though they managed to get me out in time, the damage had already been done.

When I was released six days later, my father, who was extremely concerned, asked a nurse what to expect with my future. The nurse bluntly said that I would never be a straight-A student and to expect a C average at best.

Offended, my father disregarded the insensitive remark and vowed to do everything in his power to give me every bit of love and support he could.

Quarterly check-ups revealed nothing significant; in fact, the examining physicians said I appeared to be fine. A college student, who was studying physiotherapy and renting a room in my parent's house at the time, noticed my delayed motor skills one day in our backyard and asked if he could do an examination. He concluded that I might have cerebral palsy, a term that had yet to be used to describe my situation. This prospect was shocking to my parents, considering the number of specialists and doctor appointments we had been to by that point. Soon after, my parents took me to the Children's Developmental Rehabilitation Program (CDRP) in Hamilton, Ontario, Canada, where several doctors ran a spasticity clinic, officially confirming at 16-months-old that I did, in fact, have cerebral palsy.

Since that day, not knowing that I was going to have to fight, not only to stay positive for my family and friends but mostly for myself. The occupational therapists, physiotherapists, and doctors told my parents that I may never walk or speak normally and that I would have major coordination issues. Well, it turned out I could do nearly everything and beyond with hard work and practice. Despite having articulation issues, I began to speak when most infants do, giving me a voice we were told I would never have.

I learned how to walk on my own two feet after attending the Moira Institute Program for three weeks around the age of five. Eventually, I started school and began learning just like everyone else. I participated in sports activities with my friends and joined a sports team for the disabled. I was beginning to live the life God gave me with the love and support of those around me.

I was supported by educational assistants from Kindergarten to post-secondary education who made sure I had every opportunity to succeed. In college, I made it onto the Dean's Honours List and graduated as an architectural technician with the help of technology. You might be questioning my career choice, but computers have really opened doors for people like me, allowing technology to become natural extensions of our bodies. I chose this career path because of my love of architectural design and a strong desire to build the future. With that said, the biggest challenge I face to this day isn't the ability to be able to practice my trade; it's landing gainful employment.

Graduates often spread their wings and fly into their first job. Not me. Even though I have an impressive resume outlining my expertise, I have applied to thousands of jobs I was qualified for to no avail. Getting interviews hasn't been the issue. Where it goes downhill is when they find out I have cerebral palsy. I know, I don't want to be that guy that blames their disability, but time after time, every opportunity ends the same way.

At first, I was open about my disability on my resume and would often take interviews with my parents present. This way they could help translate what I was trying to say. A career counsellor eventually suggested removing information about my disability to get more bites. It didn't matter; once they heard I was wheelchair-bound and had speech articulation issues, it was game over.

Interview after interview, it became clear that workplaces weren't accessible to the disabled. Multitasking, answering phone calls, meeting with clients, visiting job sites, I can do all these things mentally, but not physically. Many potential employers weren't even open to job modifications or an opportunity to prove myself on a volunteer basis.

It didn't take long to start feeling like a liability in every sense of the word. All I've ever needed is for someone to give me a fair chance. Just one. In truth, I find it both humbling and humiliating to still find myself searching for my first real job.

We all think about the what-ifs in life, it's hard not to, but I find it difficult not to fantasize about receiving the same opportunities able-bodied individuals are given. I don't want to be bitter, I really don't, but struggling with self-worth and frustration in a world not built for someone like me takes my mind to dark places.

As I transitioned into adulthood, my frustrations occasionally turned into full meltdowns, leaving me emotionally exhausted. I passively watched as friends and family went from being successful in their careers to dating someone and starting their own families. These were all things I wanted to do in my life too, but I just couldn't. I know if I weren't disabled, I would have at least been in a relationship because it's not my personality holding me back but my body.

I've faced a lot of rejection in my life, and dating has been no different. I've asked countless women out on dates over the years with no luck. Online dating has been great in terms of communication and widening my social circle, but the same root problems persist. I've tried to be open and honest about my disability, even though it's a turn-off for most. I've flipped back and forth between revealing my physical disability in my profile and keeping it hidden so someone could at least get to know me before passing judgement. However, both situations lead down the same path eventually.

To be honest, I don't think I can stomach another person saying, "I'm not the woman for you, but can we still be friends?" It makes me feel so defeated and unworthy. They can pull the ripcord and float away to safety, but I can't. This is me, and I'm left to deal with the emotional repercussions. As I've gotten older, I've noticed that people have become more understanding of my situation, but it's still not enough.

There's no doubt in my mind that girls find me attractive. I'm often told that it's not my disability that scares them, but it's what the future would look like in terms of caring for herself and me, having children, and life in general. That's something I totally understand. My life gave me these challenges, but how I respond to them has always been important.

Making things work has always been my goal, and I'm hoping to find someone who will be willing to take that challenge with me.

Although some of life's pleasures are not accessible to me, a part of me lives vicariously through those I love. There is no one I'm more proud of or grateful for than my friends and cousins, especially the men who are true gentlemen, husbands and fathers, giving their families the love and respect everyone deserves. These role models have my absolute respect and support, and I admire them for it.

The one thing that has really helped me these past few years has been getting involved with my friend's and cousins' children. While I may never have children of my own, I can put effort into strengthening my relationships with those around me. I get immense joy watching these kids grow up.

While I'm not the only person in the world wishing to marry or begin a family, I've come to terms that it's not the end of the world, but that doesn't mean I need to give up.

Having children of my own would be amazing, knowing it's a special gift to have one of God's blessings, and carry on my family legacy, a gift that I respect. With everything that I've faced in my life, there is one accomplishment that I'm truly proud of, and that's been publishing my own book about life with cerebral palsy. I set out to demonstrate to the world that we, the disabled community, have emotions and feelings just like everyone else. We have dreams and goals that we hope to achieve, no matter how different our bodies are, and I hope my memoir opens the hearts and minds of readers the world over.

I can honestly say that my life turned a corner after releasing my book. I've made it my goal to connect with the disabled community around the world and with parents caring for disabled children to offer answers and advice based on my experiences. Has this been my calling all along? The one thing I do know is that I simply can't give up because I'm a CP Warrior!

—

CHAPTER 6

Pets and Debts

By Mark Wood

There are certain things that can happen to you during your life, both good and less good, and the top three most stressful things sometimes come in this order: death of a loved one, moving house and divorce.

I've completed all three, plus a few others, and have the well-worn t-shirt to show for it too.

And the scars.

In fact, the scars almost feel like a badge of honour, a medal awarded for your participation in a long running campaign. They show that you have 'been there' and have faced life's greatest challenges and survived to see another day. What they never show is just how deep those wounds actually are beneath the surface and the longer lasting effects they leave you with.

Yes, people see the surface damage which, no matter how well you disguise it, still shows through.
People you haven't seen for a while meet you and say, "Gosh, you've changed, what happened?", and their friendly offer of help is well intentioned and generally welcomed, but can they actually help get you back on your feet? Do you really need their help?

Or do you have to go it alone?

Well, I am a firm believer that life is all about choices. The choices we make, the choices that others make, and the choices which are out of our hands and over which we have no control.

How can I explain this? Think about a bullseye. The centre spot, or gold, is what we have control over in our lives, those things we can choose to change immediately by ourselves.

The next circle out is those things which we can have an influence on in order to make a change, and we may be able to use someone else's help to complete this. The outermost circle is that over which we have no control or influence, and we are powerless to change anything here. I now train people to work with their mindset, acting upon only that which they can control or influence and letting anything else go, because chasing those things outside of our control and influence is the route to anxiety, fear, frustration and unfulfillment. In doing so, we have the choice to live at what I call 'Cause' and not at 'Effect'.

'Cause' is that place where we have control over our lives, and we are free to be able to choose whatever route we wish to follow. This is called 'choice'.
'Effect' is the exact opposite. We live listening to what others tell us and choose a life of compromise. Effect is a life of excuses and make do, of fitting in, and it isn't a great place to be.

It's true that we all have a certain plan mapped out for our lives, and this is what we are encouraged to aim for right from our earliest days. Do well in school, study hard, get good grades, get a good job, get a partner, kids (perhaps), nice house and car, some debt, some savings, nice holidays, a better house, and finally retirement, playing golf and buying that two-seater sports car you could never afford before.

Whilst it is true that we have made some choices getting here, this is almost a life of total 'Effect', a grey zone, a comfortable existence, with a few ups and downs, but generally stable and happy.

So, what happens when these plans get messed up, when something happens that upsets the apple cart? Should we actually plan for every eventuality, including the bad outcomes, or does that remove our spontaneity, our spark? We hear talk of Outcome Planning and Succession Planning, but do we ever consider Crisis Planning in our own lives?

I suppose that this would be called 'Health and Safety' if it was in a work environment, planning for the worst possible scenario and what to do after it occurs, or how to avoid it.

We are taught about 'Dynamic Risk Assessment', of being able to adapt to our constantly changing world, and how to alter our course of action to avoid a catastrophe, but do we ever apply this to our domestic situation?

In my previous career (I was a Police Officer) it was almost the law that you had to have a bigger house, a better car, and definitely a divorce or two. Come on, everyone in that profession has to have at least one divorce, don't they? If you didn't, it was almost like you weren't doing the job properly! I now also realise that this isn't just exclusive to Law enforcement agencies; it occurs in every other profession too, including Teaching, Finance, and Health, to name but a few.

And boy, I had one.

A divorce.

A horrible one.

One which left me traumatised with a range of emotions: grief, sadness, anger, disbelief, and finally the realisation that it would never be fixed, no matter what I thought. I had tried to make it work, but this was a choice outside of my control. As the main working partner, I was left with the house and mortgage, the majority of the pets, including a dog, two cats, Guinea Pigs and fish, and all the debts, which, due to the rules of my employment, I had no option but to continue paying.

To continue paying for something I no longer had.

My now ex-wife took the kids and moved into rented accommodation, which she had planned to do for some time. To assist her in setting up this accommodation, she took most of the furniture and belongings from the house, and I mean most. I was left with a two-seater settee, the rented TV and video player, and one knife, fork, spoon and teaspoon. I even had to ask my next-door neighbour to open a tin of tuna to make a sandwich, as all three tin openers were also taken.

And it nearly broke me.

But…

I made a choice, a choice to survive and carry on. Believe me, there were times early on that when I did eventually get some fitful sleep, I didn't want to wake up. I was dog tired all day but lay awake at night, fighting to get to sleep, only to wake feeling completely wiped out. Food was 'off the menu', as I didn't feel like eating, although my dog fared really well for a few weeks, lapping up the leftovers from meals I had hardly touched. But I did wake each day, and I kept going. Slowly, painfully sometimes, but I went through the first three months and came out alive. I was sleeping on a camp bed - not the most comfortable, I can tell you, and eventually managed to get a bed of my own, thanks to my Mum, and a bed for when the girls came to stay over.

And it actually made me a better person. The bubble burst and I took control of my life, got things organised, and carried on. The house was sold, and the equity was put into a holding account. There followed six years of sorting out bills, debts, Solicitors, rented properties and finally a new house of my own (well, mine and the Building Society!)

I now look back on this unhappy time in my life and realise that I had been bumbling along for years, being a 'please person', sticking in the Grey Zone as it was the path of least resistance. I recognised that actually, things only ever changed when I was forced outside that zone, either to a soaring high or to a crashing low, and that my personal growth and evolution actually only occurred at those extremes.

Imagine you can see a heart trace on a piece of paper like they produce when you have a cardiac incident. The grey zone is the middle bit, and the extremes are the peaks and troughs on the trace, the 'Dup' and the 'Lub' of your heartbeat.

My relationship with my ex is now much better; we get on and talk as adults with each other.

My kids are now grown with their own relationships and families, and thankfully they are not affected by what happened between their Mum and myself. I have looked back and now realise that what we had, although stable, wasn't what she wanted at that time. She has moved on, and so have I.

—

And that's the thing. There is someone out there waiting for you too, as I found out. A wonderful, kind and loving person who has restored my faith in humanity in a unique and special way. And I would never have met her unless I had gone through the break-up.

So, what did I learn from all that happened? Well, I learned that you can choose to stay where you are, wallowing in self-pity and getting the same old things. Or, you can choose to change and experience new things. I train and utilise Neuro Linguistic Programming, and there is an NLP presupposition that says, 'If you keep on doing what you've always done, you'll keep on getting what you always got'.

This means that unless you choose to change your situation, then you will carry on living in a well of personal despair. I desperately wanted to keep a hold on those things from the past and for my life to continue as it used to be, and it wasn't until I made the choice to accept what had happened and to take control of my future that I began to flourish.

My advice is this. Dwelling on the past will hold you back and tie you down to something which no longer exists, no matter how much you long for it. Make a decision, get some help, start afresh, take on a new challenge and live the best life you possibly can because no one else can do it for you.

Take control, make a change, and carry on. I have spoken to many people who have experienced severe trauma in their lives, both physical and mental, and have lived a life of 'wanting something better'. Without exception, they have all had that significant emotional event happen to them, which kickstarted their journey to recovery.

You need a lightbulb moment to happen. Look for opportunities as they present themselves to you, and grasp them tightly. Look up! If you walk along watching your feet, you will miss that butterfly or falling leaf above your head, and who knows where that might lead should you catch a glimpse of it.

CHAPTER 7

Is your Career Killing You?

By Martin Sharp

Sometimes you have to be selfish to be selfless. Yet, what does that really mean?

You have probably heard the safety briefing when flying that if you run out of oxygen yourself, you can't help anyone else with their oxygen mask. Or, put more bluntly: if you die, you can't help anyone else!

Like insurance that you don't appreciate until you need to claim from it, the universe, if you are lucky, sends you a warning shock alerting you that something needs to change before it sends the final blow. Yet how many people actually heed the warning?

The bright sun rose high in the midday sky, warming the dry air to over 28°C and baking the ground. The heat was an unusual sensation for visitors, although not for those who live here, currently wearing woollen hats, jumpers and long trousers, a stark contrast to those queuing up in shorts and t-shirts with their bronzed skin glistening in the light. In colder climates, like the UK, at the end of December, they would be snuggling down into a warm house with the wind and rain battering the outside world; this was a very welcome change.

A very welcome change indeed, as in 2014, I was 5 years into running my own business, helping my clients across the world implement their business transformations. They described me as "Knowledgeable, personable, refreshing, unbiased, diligent, helpful! A breath of fresh air in a world where complexity often seems to create as many challenges as it solves." I worked tirelessly to ensure every engagement ended with success. As a business consultant, enterprise architect and strategic thinker since 1993, when problems appeared, I'd find a solution.

As we stood in line for the Incredible Hulk roller coaster in Universal Studios theme park in Orlando, Florida, US, I wasn't working with clients. I was there as a devoted husband and father to my loving and highly supportive family, ensuring that they lived a life full of amazing experiences.

It didn't take long for us to arrive at the front of the queue. The excited anticipation of the ride was bursting from my 11 and 7-year-old. They bounced up and down, asking lots of questions. The gates opened, and we sat in the bright green car with the burgundy coloured seats. The safety bar came over our head; there was a problem; it didn't fit! "I'm sorry, sir", came the young apologetic voice of a man probably of university age wearing the park uniform, "you're going to have to wait for the next car. We have larger seats in that one."

"Hang on, larger seats? Why would I need a larger seat?" I thought as the next car arrived and we were ushered to the special section.

"I'm sorry, sir!" came the young apologetic voice for a second time "you are just too big to go on this ride!"

Devastated, I looked at my children and asked my friend Andy to take them for me, as it wasn't fair that they should miss out. As I watched from the side with my wife and parents, I imagined the loops, the twists and turns, and I could hear their laughter on the breeze as they zoomed past. They thoroughly enjoyed it!

It wasn't the last time during that 4-week family holiday over the Christmas of 2014 that I couldn't take my children on a theme park ride, and towards the end, I stopped trying.

Looking over the fantastic photos we'd taken, I was shocked to see that I had 'moobs', all 24 stone or 154kg of me. And once I recognised that, it was hard to ignore the other symptoms, the aches and pains that I'd brushed off as just getting older. The lower back problems I'd assumed came from working at the computer and sitting in various meetings. The trouble breathing even when not exerting myself, I explained as just asthma that I had since a child.

The problem was working diligently for my clients had left no time for me.

When factoring in time with the wider family, keeping up with friends and walking the dog, my self-care and personal development were pushed so far down the list it didn't really register.

I was now having to push myself out of chairs and roll onto my front to get out of bed; I no longer fitted into my kayak, a sport I'd loved since Scouts, and I no longer enjoyed cycling. I realised something had to change. I had to obtain the fitness and body that I desired, learn how to keep it that way and do all this while fitting it around my hectic schedule.

"Where to start?". Whilst I enjoyed kayaking, walking and cycling recreationally, I wasn't sporty. If you asked my mum, she would probably laugh at the idea. As a child, I would complain when we went on long walks.

The thing was, back then, I had age on my side. My growing body burnt off whatever was thrown at it, and the kayaking, walking and cycling I started to enjoy in my mid-teens was stimulus enough to keep me relatively healthy.

Though not now, the sedentary lifestyle of a desk-bound consultant and business owner kicked in for 12-14 hours per day plus travelling six days a week.

The most exercise I got was carrying around the backpack with the laptop in it wherever I went!

I said I would change and made a start getting a gym membership and a personal trainer at Virgin Active in Leeds. Downloaded a diet plan from the Internet, tracked calories on My Fitness Pal and walked 10,000 steps per day.

The thing was, none of these worked. The gym membership went barely used beyond the once per week visit to the personal trainer; even then I had an excuse. You know how it is, a deadline for this client, an issue with another client or taking onboard other people's problems, even not being in the city, county or country, which would mean I wasn't available.

When not out with clients or on other business trips, I logged 2400 calories in My Fitness Pal using its built-in calculator, which said it was what my body needed to lose weight. After reading articles on the Internet, I was aiming for a lot less. If a calorie deficit is good, then a bigger one should gain a faster result, right?

However, when on business trips, I had an excuse to join in to build rapport and make change happen, and most of these didn't get logged. The beers, the wines, the spirits, the fantastic dishes and desserts. There were lots of these as I'd be working away for 20 days a month on average.

I tried alternative exercises. Taking up Karate with my daughter, and when I was in London, joining in the weekly kickboxing session with a friend in Potter's Bar.

I tried different diets like the South Beach, Weight Watchers, Mediterranean, Atkins, volumetric and other things I found on the Internet or was recommended to do. I joined accountability groups, and I created one with my friends James and Vish. I paid thousands to gain results, yet nothing stuck. Nothing could marry my commitment to my family, clients, or friends with that of shifting my weight.

The only thing that happened regularly was the 10,000 steps per day as I shuffled around the offices between meetings. As you can imagine, my results were poor, only dropping 10kg over the five years.

The worst thing was, I considered this would be me forever. I was happy with life, cheerful and successful, so it wasn't a bad thing. I just hoped I wouldn't become a burden to my family and friends too quickly if my health deteriorated.

Over breakfast, in the Crowne Plaza Hotel Felbridge, near Gatwick airport on the 26th May 2019, James and I were chatting when a sharp looking gentleman in a well-fitted suit, glasses and with a chiselled look asked, "Can I join you for breakfast?"

"Certainly, it would be great", we responded over our cooked full English breakfast of sausage, bacon, eggs, beans, fried slice, tomatoes and mushrooms as he seated himself next to us, fresh coffee in hand.

It wasn't long before the conversation turned to health and fitness "so how do you keep yourself looking so well, Pete?" James enquired.

"Funny you should ask that. I used to be quite big back in the day and tried everything, and I couldn't find anything that would work until I started working with an online coach." It must have been the sceptical look on our faces that caused Pete to pull out his phone, and my jaw visibly dropped as he showed us photos of someone similar though twice his current size, along with pictures of a recent photoshoot he'd taken part in.

As fate would have it, his online coach, Adam, was also at this same event, and Pete offered to introduce us. Adam is a bodybuilder turned world's leading online physique and lifestyle consultant whose aim is not just about transforming physique; it's about transforming lives, and he has a library of case studies to prove that it works. He said to me, "You have to find the mental strength to change and make this one of your highest values for your transformation to succeed."

I thought about it for a moment, about what it really meant. Was he saying that I had to start putting myself first to be able to change?

It dawned on me that he was right. I had to be selfish to be selfless, and I couldn't work on myself alongside everything else as I had been trying to do.

I had to work on myself FOR everything else! For my family that I love dearly. For my friends that I like spending time with and supporting. For my clients who needed their results.

All I needed was a plan to run my change like I had done any other successful business transformation. I signed up for a professional custom personal training and nutrition plan. Then started to work out how I would fit the plan into my already rammed schedule.

To learn how to adapt it to work wherever I was, whether working out in luxury, well-equipped gyms like those in Dubai or basic basement gyms in Romania, rooftop gyms in the Czech Republic or the well-equipped and busy PureGym in my home town in the UK.

It wasn't easy, although in the first 12 weeks, despite being away from home for eight of them, six of them out of the country, I'd dropped over 10kg (22lb). With further learning and adaptions, managing nutrition and exercise while away, even when there were no gyms, the following three months saw another 7kg down. My suits no longer fitted, I looked like a young kid playing dress-up with his dads' clothes, and I had to start replacing my wardrobe on a regular basis.

When the gyms were closed because of lockdown, I had to quickly build a makeshift gym at home - acquiring equipment from friends, eBay, and Facebook.

I was learning how to further adapt to working out at home because I pinned my health and progress to my highest values, giving me perseverance and a plan to succeed by building consistency of results.

People I've known for years pass me by as they don't recognise me as within one year, I dropped 40kg, despite the travel, client engagements, and COVID lockdown effects.

The most dramatic effects are not those you can externally see. Because I'm no longer just existing in life for others, now I'm living my life for myself.

Capable of cycling for miles if I choose. I can perform handstands again when I want, though I am unsure how useful that is in a meeting! Feeling renewed and more confident, like the more youthful version of myself, I know makes a big difference in everything I do.

Now I share this knowledge with others after obtaining recognised qualifications in health and sports science. I asked Adam to mentor me to help achieve these transformative changes for others, and have become a member of the Chartered Institute for the Management of Sport and Physical Activity.

What lights me up more than anything is the joy I hear as others enjoy newfound freedom, confidence and happiness from health and fitness.

At that moment, the kids join in by policing their dad's Haribo habit and changing their and his association with food. The time a mum makes time for herself and renews her hobby of hill walking. That excited message that they could play tennis again or do the monkey bars for the first time or go out to play frisbee in the park.

CHAPTER 8

A Little Help from my Friends

By Phil Horrod

Have you ever felt really sad, anxious, or stressed out about something?

If so, what did you do about it?

Did you keep it to yourself and just hope the feeling would go away by itself, or did you reach out to someone and ask them for help?

If you're like most of the population, you probably kept things to yourself and didn't talk to anyone at all.

A study undertaken by the World Health Organisation found that up to 80% of people who experience any kind of mental health challenge don't seek help or treatment. This includes 50% of people with Bipolar disorder, 55% of people with panic disorder, 56% of people experiencing major depression and an unbelievable 78% of people with alcohol use disorder.

So why is this a subject of interest to me?

Well, in 2014, I was diagnosed as being Bipolar after experiencing a life-changing stress-related breakdown, which left me hospitalised, unable to work and almost lost me my family, my home and even my life.

Mental Health has therefore been high on my agenda ever since. Not just my own, but the mental health of society in general and how we seem to allow ourselves to approach it differently to physical health.

So why do so many people not seek help when they find themselves struggling? If they broke an arm, had a deep cut that needed stitches, or were in severe pain, most sensible people would immediately take a trip to the hospital, or their GP, to seek some sort of help for whatever injury they'd sustained. So why isn't the same true when someone finds themselves with a mental health problem rather than a physical one?

There are many potential reasons for this, but most are likely to be connected in some way to factors such as:

- The stigma, which unfortunately still surrounds mental health conditions
- A lack of knowledge around being able to recognise the symptoms of mental health problems
- Fear of what potential treatments may include
- Anosognosia is a condition experienced by about half the people with schizophrenia and other psychotic disorders. Essentially, these

people are so impaired by their illness that they are completely unaware there's anything wrong with them at all

So what can we do to try and counter this major problem of people's reluctance to seek out help for mental health related challenges?

At a global level, the Covid pandemic has started to make mental health challenges more recognised and talked about. This is particularly the case by those in influential positions, such as the medical profession, politicians and celebrity role models, who have thankfully started to speak out about the importance of maintaining good mental health, as well as about their own personal mental health challenges.

In the UK, we have also seen a huge public outcry over our collective concern about what impact the pandemic may have had on our children's mental health. This is something close to my own heart, given we have two young teenage children who have both been impacted very differently by their respective experiences of the pandemic.

Thankfully, this increased openness has begun to make it less of a stigma to talk about mental health, although we still have a long way to go before mental health is spoken about anywhere near as openly as it needs to be.

As well as being more open to discussing mental health at a national level, we also need to consider how we approach this at a personal level. Are we personally comfortable talking about our own mental health, are we happy to ask someone we know about their own mental wellbeing, and are we more open to seeking out help when we find ourselves struggling in some way?

I'm really passionate about how we can better encourage people to reach out for help when they need it. This is partly as a result of me realising I had previously held double standards around being open about my own mental health situation. I had been fine to seek medical help for our son, who was later diagnosed with ADHD. However, when it came to myself after my burnout, I was initially completely reluctant to talk to anyone about my mental health challenges.

I've since become a great believer that seeking out help for a mental health challenge should be no more difficult than when we need to reach out for help when it's required for a physical health problem.

With the benefit of hindsight, the main thing that got me through and kept me from taking my own life through deep depression was that I eventually asked for the help I desperately needed from the medical profession, my family and my friends.

In the past, I'd grown up where the general approach taken by society was pretty much that anyone who needed to reach out for help was showing a weak side to their character. Very much along the lines of the old belief that 'real men don't cry' and that men in particular just need to keep a 'stiff upper lip'.

In reality, when I fell ill, I actually found the complete opposite to be true: asking for help was actually a sign of strength, not weakness. Bottling things up inside and not talking about them just made things much worse; talking with others about what I was experiencing really helped. Taking this approach is much more like the belief that 'a trouble shared is a trouble halved'.

When I later came to reflect on this aspect of how we normally respond to mental health challenges, I realised how over the years, music and certain songs have played a large part in showing us we need to be more open to seeking out and accepting help and support.

Think of the messages given in the lyrics of some really well-known songs. We often listen to these in a way that we may just take on board the tune and perhaps the words of the song, but not always the important message which lies behind the lyrics.

Examples of what I mean are:
" I get by with a little help from my friends"
" I'll be there for you, 'cause you're there for me too"

"You just call out my name and you know wherever I am I'll come running"

Of course, there are also many religious songs and hymns that encourage us to seek help and give up our worries, concerns, and prayers to some higher power than ourselves. An example of this is the hymn we sang at my mum's funeral after she passed away when I was just 12. We sang Psalm 23 from the King James Bible.

We all go through life's journey with all its's ups and downs. Some of these downs might be the times when we lose a loved one, maybe lose our job, separate from our partner, or perhaps experience a different type of traumatic life event.

Whichever of these we experience, it will cause us to have a level of emotional pain and give rise to us having a mental and emotional health challenge.

Sometimes, if we're lucky, this might be short-lived. At other times, the effects of our experience can affect us for years, decades, or even for the rest of our life.

Whatever situation you happen to find yourself in, try your best to reach out for help as soon as you can, whether this is to a friend, a family member, someone in the medical profession, or to whoever or whatever you believe in as being a greater power than yourself.

If you do, you'll find you can always get by with a little help from your friends!

Stay safe and healthy, mentally as well as physically.

CHAPTER 9

Don't Give Up

By Sam Ortyl

The most challenging time of my life was during the period of eight years when I suffered from severe anxiety, panic attacks, periods of depression and substance abuse. All that led me to almost complete self-destruction and being close to suicide.

I spent a lot of time figuring out how I got myself to the point where feelings of impending doom and drinking myself to oblivion became integral parts of my daily life.

Unsurprisingly, I think it all started when I was growing up. I was always this scrawny little guy with a happy-go-lucky attitude who just wanted everyone to get along. In my school years, I was quite shy, I didn't get into many fights, and I was always lacking confidence and self-esteem. Growing up without a father, in a family with constant financial challenges, instilled in me a strong feeling of inferiority.

This may seem like it is unrelated, but it all manifested later in my life as a number of different unhealthy coping mechanisms and behaviours that developed into anxiety and panic attacks.

When I started experiencing my first panic attacks, I had no idea what it was. The feeling came out of nowhere, and for no apparent reason, it was very strange. I felt that my chest was getting very tight, my heartbeat would speed up, and my blood pressure would get so high that I felt like my head was going to explode. Like many men, I chose to "man up", ignore the problem and soldier on with my daily activities.

I was always very keen on having a few drinks, but over time it became my (very unhealthy) coping mechanism. With the passing months and years, my anxiety and panic attacks got more severe, and I drank more and more to help myself "cure" the problem.

Looking back at that whole situation, I am very surprised I managed to pretend that everything was alright for so long. I became a master of hiding my pain and suffering. I would never admit that my drinking got a bit out of control.

If you have never experienced a panic attack, I can tell you that it feels like you're going to die and make a fool out of yourself in the process. Your heart rate speeds up, your chest tightens, you can't take a proper breath, your palms start to sweat, your body starts to shake, and you just want to run away. Sounds like "fun", right? It's one of the most horrible feelings that you can imagine.

With time my panic attacks got so bad that if I felt one coming on a train or a bus, I had to leave at the next stop regardless of how far I was from my destination. I had a strong feeling that I had to run away from that situation and place or something bad was going to happen. Usually, I would get off and direct my steps straight to the convenience store and get a few beers to help me feel a bit better.

That was my coping mechanism for years.

As I found out from my experience, the biggest problem with trying to use alcohol as a "cure" is it only brings temporary relief, and when the effects wear off, your anxiety (or other issues) come back with stronger force. Over time this creates a totally insane self-perpetuating cycle of substance abuse, self-destruction, self-hatred and feeling of hopelessness.

One of the first things that helped me understand what I was really going through and turn things around was a book, "Panic attacks" by Christine Ingham. The book still sits unfinished on my shelf to this day. I stopped reading at the part when she helped me understand that having panic attacks is an indication that something in your life is not working well. I started examining my life and realised that many things were not working well, but at that time, I had no idea what to do to improve my situation and how to ask for help. I continued my struggle for another year or so until I smashed my face into the proverbial rock bottom.

It all started innocently, I just wanted to have a few drinks on Friday evening, but it quickly got out of control and turned into a few days of heavy drinking that I could not stop. It got to the point where I would wake up only to drink half of glass of straight vodka to help me soothe my anxiety a bit, so I could go back to sleep. On day four or five (I can't even remember), I realised that I was going down very fast, and if I didn't do something about this situation, it would not end well for me.

I somehow found enough courage to pull myself together and go to the hospital to ask for help. I felt that I was at the end of the road, and this was my only option. As I walked to the nearest hospital, my mind started creating this amazing vision that I would be admitted to the ward, stay there for a few days, get a nice fruit salad and a magic drip with vitamin mix and go home feeling like new.

Luckily for me, nothing like that happened. As I walked into the intensive care unit, I managed to mumble something along the lines of "I have difficulty breathing, I think I have alcohol poisoning".

The nurses took it very seriously and decided to get an ambulance to send me to another hospital with an A&E. The journey there was horrible; I was sitting at the back with a paramedic, and we were both silent most of the way.

I was looking at the floor feeling ashamed, guilty, embarrassed, hopeless, and totally stupid.

I felt like I was wasting resources; I felt I like these guys could have used their time and ambulance to save someone's life. I didn't realise that they were actually saving mine.

The waiting room was packed when we have arrived at the A&E. When the effects of your heavy drinking are wearing off, and your anxiety is coming back, the last thing you want to do, is to be in a room full of people. You want to hide somewhere in the corner, not being visible to anyone, just to try to find a little bit of peace and silence so that you can somehow deal with all the anxious feeling creeping up on you.

After the initial health check, I was sent to the psych ward as I admitted to having suicidal thoughts. I will never forget walking there behind a nurse who did not say a word to me. It was like a scene from a movie. We had to walk through a corridor that connected two parts of the hospital. It was already late, and the dark corridor was brightened by the moonlight which found its way through the big windows. That was my turn around point; at that moment, I realised that it's all up to me to clean up this mess that I created in my life. I have realised that it was all up to me to clean up this mess that I have created and that nobody was coming to save me, and I had to take responsibility for everything I was going through.

My chat with the psychiatrist was brief.

I told him what happened, asked him for a few sleeping pills and told him that I'd be good as new after a solid nap.

The following day the real struggle began. The effects of all the alcohol wore off, and anxiety hit me back again like a ton of bricks. The first few days were terrible; I could barely get through it. I asked a girl that I was dating at that time to come and spend a few days with me. I told her the whole story over the phone, and she came to help me out. When she walked into my place, I gave her a big hug and started weeping like a little baby; everything came out, I could not hold it any longer. Until this day, I am trying to figure out if that moment was harder for her or me.

That trip to the hospital really triggered something in my mind. I did not want to find myself in the same situation again, and I was ready to do anything it took to keep that promise to myself. I started taking my life apart, identifying things that did not work well and realised that I had to make significant changes to create a different life for myself.

One of the biggest influences on my recovery was exercise. I would go to the gym regularly to burn all the excess energy, get rid of all my negative emotions and create a stronger mind. It became my coping mechanism.

I did everything I could to stay busy from the moment I woke up until I went to bed. That helped me keep all the distractions away, stay focused on the recovery and create a new life for myself.

Every morning right after I woke up, I would put my headphones on and listen to a motivational speech that helped me create a positive mindset for the day and stay focused on the important things. That is something that I still do most days.

Eventually, I moved to a different town, changed my job and started spending my time with different people. I became very aware of what I was reading, watching and listening to. Everything about my life has changed, and I was very careful how I was spending my time.

From listening to my favourite motivational speakers like Tony Robbins, Les Brown, Nick Vujicic and Jim Rohn, I got introduced to coaching and fell in love with the idea. I decided to take that path, and after a year or so of studying and practising, I became a certified Transformational Life Coach. It was very fulfilling to help someone else explore their thoughts and feelings to be able to overcome obstacles, and move forward with their life. With time, I became more drawn towards facilitating workshops and public speaking. I have realised that teaching gives me the most satisfaction and fulfilment. I love creating a space where people can feel safe and comfortable, be able to share and discuss ideas, and learn from each other.

Mental health naturally became the subject of my focus. I wanted to use the personal experience and knowledge I have gained on my journey to teach other people how they can better look after themselves and overcome adversity in their personal life. Now I really enjoy delivering First Aid for Mental Health courses for individuals and businesses, which teach people how to recognise that someone might be going through challenges with their mental health and what you can do to support them. These learning experiences not only give people a better understanding of the subject of mental health but also teach the practical skills that can be used to support someone in crisis.

I went through a lot of suffering that did not make sense at the time, but it totally does now. I understand that I had to go through all those experiences to get to where I am, to become who I am and find my purpose and meaning in life. The most challenging days of my life led me to the most beautiful experiences. I had an opportunity to meet a lot of amazing people, do things that I never thought were possible for me and discover that I could create a better life with meaning and purpose.

If you are going through something challenging right now, please don't give up on yourself. Keep going, ask for help, be kind to yourself and believe that better days are coming… because they are.

CHAPTER 10

Triumph Against the Odds

By Satwinder Sagoo

"The only limitations in life are the limitations you keep affirming in your head."

This quote could not be any truer because, in life, we are born to create the very fortunes we aspire to.

I want you to think about something for a minute - how strong is your faith in yourself and belief in your abilities? There is always one obstacle, either physically or mentally, stopping us from pushing ourselves to the max and achieving those huge goals, but the rule is always the same - it's not your situation, but how you respond to it that truly counts.

What CHOICE do you make - give up and try something new or keep persisting until you succeed? If we choose the former, we would be forever trying out new things with no joy, whilst others who are more persistent command and conquer.

If anyone ever feels their physical limitations will stop them from enjoying their life to the max just ask Nic Vujicic. Nic was born with no arms and legs, yet still rides horses, swims, plays golf and does bungee jumping.

He is also a man I had the privilege of sharing the platform with in Passion Vista's latest nominations of Global men to look up to in 2021.

Another fine example is Jessica Cox, a woman who was born with no arms, yet learned how to fly a plane, drive a car and play the piano. She was also the first armless black belt in American Taekwondo.

What these inspiring people demonstrate is that if you look past your physical limits, you don't just make the seemingly impossible possible, but you also inspire others to push beyond their own limitations.

My big toes are inverted, and my second toes nearly overlap the third ones. I'm also flat-footed. My feet have been this way since childhood. Yet, just like Nic Vujicic, I never let these limitations beat me; I chose to COMMAND and CONQUER!

My childhood days at school were quite treacherous, to say the least. I was badly bullied; many mocked me for my good nature and told me that my feet made me look like an elf. Many times I would walk home in fear expecting other students to wait for me and gang up on me, and 75% of the time, my fears were right. I was even followed to the toilet with students threatening to climb over and look at me whilst I was using it, or punching and kicking the door while I was in...all because of the state of my feet, it simply gave them fuel to make a mockery of me.

After a lot of thought and courage, I started Karate when I was 11 to improve my self-confidence. The state of my feet didn't allow me to hop or even run fast, let alone jump. I started to enjoy Karate so much - until it came to doing jump kicks. When the instructor gave the count, I could barely hop, whilst others were jumping nice and high doing their kicks.

As the weeks of training went on, I got more and more frustrated until, eventually, I got so frustrated I walked out of the class in tears. I just could not jump kick, and I told my mum, "I'm not going back". But she talked to me and told me I should keep trying and that I would eventually find a way. So back I went, I apologised to the instructor and told him of my situation, and after speaking, we found a way to progress with my jump kicks. So back I trained, yet I was still experiencing pain as I was jumping a little.

However...

Was I going to give my critics the victory they craved for? NEVER! It was time to change that story from one I hated to the one I desired. It was time to create a special new chapter in my life, a chapter I could be truly proud of and help others in a similar position to myself.

With the help of my instructor, I persisted; I found a way around my restrictions through more advanced stretching techniques along with jump drills, and from the point of not being able to hop, I was starting to slowly but surely do jump kicks.

The feel-good factor pushed me to do more, and gradually my feet became more flexible and conditioned to help me push past my limiting beliefs. I was starting to feel a bit more confident going to school against the bullies and my home times were less fearful.

As time went on, I started to enter Karate competitions in both fighting and demonstrations (also known as Kata) and won trophies. I then began to teach other students how to grow their confidence, execute techniques sharply and have faith in themselves when doubt started to creep in. Eventually, I would work myself up to a 2nd Dan Black belt in Karate.

As you do in life, I got married, moved house and had a new job. Attending Karate classes became more difficult, and I also wanted to learn a different art suited to the street style, so I went for Jujitsu, which involves self-defence and throwing. As I progressed, I would achieve a black belt in this martial art too, again overlooking the limitations of my toes to perform techniques crisply and sharply.

So, 30 years in martial arts, that persistence, that belief, that tenacity and dedication to keep training even when I felt I couldn't, led me to be the holder of not one but TWO black belt certificates...in Karate and Jujitsu.

With my feet now fully conditioned, despite their poor structure, I am now training in Stunt martial arts, which teaches you to do the fancy tricks and flips you see in films. Will it be easy? No, it won't. I am 42 and not quite able to do the splits, though I am centimetres away from completing a full side split. Will it be worth it? You bet it will!

I can now also do a fast, one-handed cartwheel working into an aerial cartwheel. I have not once used my age as an excuse to quit on my goals. I am consistently working away, learning new ways to develop and train in order to reach my goals, to achieve my aim of doing motivational martial arts stunt reels with motivational captions on my YouTube channel and website.

The great Jeff Olsen said that some things are "easy to do, and easy not to do." It was just as easy for me to quit martial arts altogether, as it was to focus on my possibilities and break free from that mental prison cell. Breaking free and overcoming my fears has led to endless creative opportunities that would not have been possible had I listened to both my inner and outer demons.

Never let your restrictions or your critics dictate what you can and can't do. If you look hard enough and work with the right people, you will find a way through even the toughest physical challenges.

Whatever the challenge, don't quit - keep going, and NEVER GIVE UP. Take each challenge as an opportunity to grow and flip your stories to the dream outcome you've always wanted to happen. Be brave enough to act out that "desires chapter" because this is your movie, and you are the star...

THIS IS YOUR LIFE!

EPILOGUE

Thank you for purchasing a copy of this book.

I hope you were able to find strength by reading the stories of others and sharing their experiences. If you are currently going through any of the experiences you've read within this book, please know that there is light at the end of the tunnel, although it probably doesn't feel like that at this point.

Look at the reflections from the Authors in here and try and find some answers for your own situation.

If you would like to share your own story, please do contact us for details on how you can take part in further volumes of this anthology.

If you enjoyed this book, we would love a review on Amazon.

Thank you again for taking the time to read our journeys.

REFERENCES / BIBLIOGRAPHY

Jeffers, S., (2007) Feel the Fear and Do It Anyway. Vermillion: London

Smith, A., (2014) Minha metade silenciosa. Gutenberg

The Gospel of John. New International Version. New International Version, NIV Copyright

1973, 1978, 1984, 2011 by Biblica, Inc.

PREVIEW OF PREVIOUS BOOKS:

Stories from Around the Globe (Volume One)

My One-Way Ticket Out by Sarah Ross

Room Five at the orphanage was a room unlike any I had ever spent time in before. It's where 20 children who were left alone by the world lived. More than half of them were abandoned by their parents. They often had a medical condition their parents couldn't afford to care for or chose not to bother with. There was a minimal level of care for them. They were given food, shelter, clothing, and medical care. They were safe. Yet, there was something powerful about Room Five that I just couldn't ignore, so I became their regular volunteer for three months.

For eight hours a day, five days a week, my purpose was to care for those forgotten children. And as the days and months passed, my spirit for life found its way back to me. I painted their nails, blew up balloons and sharpened their pencils. I played with their pet rocks with them and bought socks and hats for them, both items which are rarely donated. We built Lego towers and destroyed them, always with a laugh or cheer. When we were allowed, weather permitting, we went outside so they could breathe fresh air, and I did what I could to keep them away from rats and open sewage drains.

ABOUT THE BOOK CREATOR

Sharon Brown moved to the West Midlands in 2003 from Glasgow in Scotland. After a wide-ranging career in Event Management, Marketing, Project Management and board level support in various different industries, Sharon's passion around organising events led her to launch Lydian Events Ltd in 2015 whilst still working full time.

In 2017 Sharon took the plunge and left her corporate position to move into Self-employment full time. It wasn't long after this that Sharon soon realised the way business was heading and decided to launch an online platform for women in business in 2018 called Revival Sanctuary with the aim of connecting women globally in order to find collaborative projects to work together and build each other up.

In 2021, Sharon changed the name of her business to Lydian Group Ltd which supports four online platforms. She no longer organises corporate events and has now found a real passion for helping small business owners avoid the mistakes she made at the start and raising their profiles through writing, speaking, publishing and community opportunities.

SERVICES

MO2VATE Magazine | The Winning Formula
mo2vatemagazine.com |
editor@mo2vatemagazine.com
A global publication which highlights the writing ability and knowledge around business, health and inspirational stories of small business owners the world over.

THE BOOK CHIEF | Ignite Your Writing
Thebookchief.com | sharon@thebookchief.com
An affordable and full service to get your manuscript edited, typeset and published through a recognised brand with a niche in collaborative books.

THE SPEAKERS INDEX | Amplify Your Voice
Thespeakersindex.com |
sharon@thespeakersindex.com
A speakers and event organiser directory and magazine to allow you to get in front of the right people.

REVIVAL SANCTUARY | Women in business
Revivalsanctuary.co.uk |
sharon@revivalsanctuary.co.uk
Exclusive Private Membership Club for women in business. It attracts women who are comfortable in their own skin, supportive of other women and those willing to empower and collaborate with each other.

Printed in Great Britain
by Amazon

81639962R00068